Gilbert & Sullivan for Singers

Tenor

Edited by Richard Walters

Laura Ward, piano

To access companion recorded accompaniments online, visit:
www.halleonard.com/mylibrary

3489-0285-2010-2361

Cover illustration: W.S. Gilbert created line drawings to accompany his librettos. His childhood nickname was Bab (derived from "baby"), and this was the name he signed to the drawings. They have become known as the "Bab Illustrations." From *The Pirates of Penzance*, a dejected Frederic contemplates his misfortune at the lines, "Pour, oh, pour the pirate sherry; Fill, oh, fill the pirate glass."

ISBN 978-0-634-06015-1

HAL•LEONARD®
CORPORATION

7777 W. BLUEMOUND RD. P.O. BOX 13819 MILWAUKEE, WI 53213

Visit Hal Leonard Online at
www.halleonard.com

W.S. Gilbert

Arthur Sullivan

Contents

Though this role is usually sung by a baritone, it is possible (because of optional notes) for it to be sung by a tenor; this song appears in both the Tenor and Baritone/Bass volumes of the series.

The price of this publication includes access to companion recorded accompaniments online, for download or streaming, using the unique code found on the title page. Visit **www.halleonard.com/mylibrary** and enter the access code.

Plot Notes

THE GONDOLIERS

or *The King of Barataria*

First produced at the Savoy Theatre, London, on December 7, 1889, with an initial run of 554 performances.

Twenty-four Venetian flower girls are arranging the bouquets they will present to Marco and Giuseppe, the handsomest of all the gondoliers, in hopes of snagging a marriage proposal. The gondoliers decide to choose their brides via a game of blindman's-buff. Happily they end up with the girls they most wanted—Marco with Gianetta and Giuseppe with Tessa. A gondola arrives carrying the Plaza-Toro family. The penniless Duke of Plaza-Toro tells his daughter, Casilda, that as a baby she was married by proxy to the infant son of the King of Barataria. (Casilda loves the drummer Luiz.) The King's Grand Inquisitor objected to the monarch's religious practices, so he kidnapped the infant prince and took him to Venice to be raised by a gondolier. The prince, who does not know he is a prince, is now himself working as a gondolier in Venice. The court of Barataria has all been killed, and this gondolier is now king, if he can be found. The two newlywed couples return. The Grand Inquisitor is certain that one of the men, Marco or Giuseppe, is the King he seeks, although he can't say which, and takes them both back to Barataria. They will rule jointly until the King's old nursemaid, who is the mother of Luiz, can determine which is the real King.

Act II opens in the Court of Barataria, where the democratic leanings of the joint Kings are immediately apparent. As Giuseppe describes in **"Rising Early in the Morning,"** the Kings toil all day for their kingdom. They miss their brides. Marco describes the ladies' delicate charms in **"Take a Pair of Sparkling Eyes."** The brides appear, unable to bear the separation any longer. When the Grand Inquisitor arrives, he explains that this sort of thing had been tried once before to no good end. The Duke arrives with Casilda, who is technically married to one of the two Kings, and Luiz. The three brides ponder the predicament of their two husbands and Casilda's mother tells of her own marriage. The Grand Inquisitor brings in Inez, the nursemaid, to identify the real King. She confesses that when the King was kidnapped she tricked the Grand Inquisitor by substituting her own son. One of the "Kings" is the son of the gondolier Palmieri, the other is the son of the nurse-maid Inez, and the rightful King is Luiz! So the two Kings are gondoliers once again, each happily married to his love. Luiz, now the rightful King, and Casilda happily must be married.

HMS PINAFORE

or *The Lass that Loved a Sailor*

First produced at the Opéra Comique, London, on May 25, 1878, with an initial run of 571 performances.

On the *Pinafore*, anchored off Portsmouth, the crew is proudly polishing and scrubbing the vessel as this satire on British class distinctions and military life opens. A woman named Little Buttercup comes aboard to sell them ribbons and lace for their sweethearts. Despite her merry demeanor, she carries a mysterious secret. Sailor Ralph Rackstraw, the smartest man in the fleet, declares his love for a young maiden, with **"A Maiden Fair to See."** That maiden, unfortunately, is the Captain's daughter. The sailor Dick Deadeye appears with the unkindly explanation that Captains' daughters do not marry mere sailors. Enter the Captain. He explains to Little Buttercup that he is worried because his daughter, Josephine, has refused to marry Sir Joseph Porter, First Lord of the Admiralty. Josephine herself enters, declaring her love for a sailor aboard Pinafore. After her father explains the class issues involved with her romance she promises to forsake the sailor and reconsider Sir Joseph. Ralph finally summons the courage to confess his love to Josephine, only to have her respond coldly. A heartbroken Ralph threatens to shoot himself, but Josephine relents and confesses that she indeed loves him.

As Act II begins, the Captain paces the deck by night, singing **"Fair Moon, to Thee I Sing."** He confesses his love for Little Buttercup but quickly explains that their different social positions make a relationship impossible. Little Buttercup cryptically advises him not to be too sure of that. Sir Joseph and Josephine enter. Sir Joseph is convinced that Josephine is intimidated by his high social standing; all the while she plots her elopement with Ralph. The evil Dick Deadeye informs the Captain of Josephine's upcoming elopement, allowing the Captain to stop the marriage. The crew steps in on Ralph's behalf, but the Captain curses at this behavior, which brings Sir Joseph out of the woodwork to berate him for speaking so rudely to a British sailor. Once Sir Joseph realizes his love intended to elope with Ralph, he orders the young sailor confined below decks. At the last moment Little Buttercup brings out the truth of her mysterious secret. Apparently she once worked as a nanny of sorts, and made a terrible mistake through which two babies were mixed up. Those babies were the Captain and Ralph. So, in fact, the Captain is a mere sailor and Ralph is the Captain. Her news rings in a happy ending, as Ralph and Josephine, as well as the Captain and Little Buttercup, are freed from social restrictions and may marry.

IOLANTHE
or *The Peer and the Peri*
First produced at the Savoy Theatre, London, on November 25, 1882, with an initial run of 398 performances.

The lovely fairy women of Arcadia are unhappy in this satire on the House of Lords, because the Fairy Queen has banished Iolanthe for marrying a human. The Queen, who is secretly in love with a human named Private Willis, eventually relents and pardons Iolanthe. Iolanthe returns, looking like a young woman of 17 even though she has a 25-year-old son. Her son, Strephon, is planning to marry Phyllis, the young ward of the Lord Chancellor. But the couple has not received his blessing. The Lord Chancellor and a chorus of nobles march about demanding respect and fanfare. The Lord Chancellor loves Phyllis himself, but fearing the marriage would not be proper he asks the nobles if one of them might marry her. Lord Tolloller exalts the nobles' station, singing **"Spurn Not the Nobly Born."** Phyllis announces her objection, adding that her heart has already been given to another. Strephon enters at that moment and announces that he is the object of her affection but the Chancellor dashes his hopes. When Strephon tells his mother of these goings-on, she takes him in her arms to comfort him. Phyllis sees Strephon in the arms of this apparent 17-year-old. Certain she has been betrayed, she becomes engaged to two noblemen. As the act comes to an end, the Fairy Queen decides to send Strephon to Parliament to make nobles out of commoners and generally make life miserable for the Lord Chancellor and the other nobles.

Act II opens on the Westminster Palace Yard. Strephon has caused an uproar in Parliament, whimsically passing pointless laws. The peers appeal to the fairies. They offer no help but find the peers quite attractive. Despite her love for Willis, the Fairy Queen scolds them for even thinking about marrying mortals. Phyllis meanwhile finds her two fiancées equally uninteresting so she tells them she will choose the one who will forsake his title and give his wealth to the Irish tenantry, which neither will do. Strephon eventually convinces Phyllis that Iolanthe is really his mother and they plan to marry immediately. The Lord Chancellor has in the meantime convinced himself that it be acceptable for him to marry his ward. But Iolanthe steps forward to confess that she is his long-lost wife. The Queen is about to order Iolanthe's execution for this marriage, when the fairies step forward to announce they have all married nobles. To save them all from execution, the Lord Chancellor rewrites the law so that any fairy who does not marry a mortal will be condemned to death. The Queen happily marries Private Willis to save her own life. Wings sprout from the nobles' shoulders as the House of Peers becomes the House of Peri.

THE MIKADO
or *The Town of Titipu*
First produced at the Savoy Theatre, London, on March 14, 1885, with an initial run of 672 performances.

The setting for this most popular of Savoy operettas is the courtyard of the Japanese Lord High Executioner in the town of Titipu. Handsome Nanki-Poo runs in looking for the lovely Yum-Yum, explaining his appearance with **"A Wand'ring Minstrel."** He has loved Yum-Yum for a long time and now that Ko-Ko, Yum-Yum's guardian and fiancée, is to be beheaded he sees his opportunity. However, Ko-Ko has been reprieved, and enters to announce his new appointment as Lord High Executioner. As he discusses his wedding plans, Yum-Yum and two school-mates enter. Nanki-Poo apologizes to Ko-Ko for being in love Yum-Yum, receiving forgiveness. Later, Yum-Yum confesses to Nanki-Poo that she does not love Ko-Ko. Nanki-Poo confesses that he is actually son of the Mikado and is traveling in disguise to avoid marrying an elderly woman who mistook his good nature for affectionate advances. The Mikado meanwhile has sent word to Ko-Ko that if he doesn't execute someone soon his title will be abolished and the town reduced to a mere village. Ko-Ko spots Nanki-Poo about to end his life over his hopeless love, and asks if he might execute him since the lad is about do himself in anyway. Nanki-Poo agrees on the condition that he be allowed to marry Yum-Yum and live with her for one month before the execution. Ko-Ko agrees, being a more practical than romantic man. When Katisha, the elderly woman who wants to marry Nanki-Poo, arrives and tries to tell everyone of his true identity, she is ignored.

Act II opens on the preparations for Yum-Yum's wedding. Obsessed with her own beauty, she wonders why she should be so much more attractive than anyone else. But happiness dims when Ko-Ko learns that by law she, as the widow of Nanki-Poo, must be buried alive following his execution. A bribe to the Pooh-Bah (also known as the Lord High Everything Else) to fake a certificate of execution seems the best course of action until the Mikado arrives. When Katisha sees the execution certificate and tells the Mikado that his son has been executed, the Mikado promises punishment to all involved. Ko-Ko goes to Nanki-Poo for advice. Nanki-Poo advises him to marry Katisha. Ko-Ko woos her with the tale of a dicky-bird that died of a broken heart, and soon the two join in duet and then in marriage. Nanki-Poo, now free from Katisha's clutches, comes out of hiding and introduces the Mikado to his new daughter-in-law and thus ends the threat of punishment and the operetta.

THE PIRATES OF PENZANCE
or *The Slave of Duty*
One performance, for copyright purposes, was given on December 30, 1879, at the Royal Bijou Theatre in Paighton, Devonshire. It opened officially for a run in New York at the Fifth Avenue Theatre on December 31, 1879. The London premiere was at the Opéra Comique on April 3, 1880, with an initial run of 363 performances.

Pirate festivities on the Cornwall coast open this satire on British military and constabulary, celebrating the completion of young Frederic's pirate internship. But Frederic is dejected. His situation is explained by Ruth, who had been his nursemaid. It seems that Ruth, being quite hard of hearing, mistook Frederic's father's instruction to apprentice him as a pilot and instead set him up as a pirate. The heartbroken Frederic must, for duty's sake, return to the honest world and work to end piracy even though this means betraying his pirate friends. He begs the pirates to give up their life of crime but they decline. Ruth begs Frederic to take her with him, as he has never seen another woman and considers the aging Ruth to be beautiful. Just then a party of beautiful young maidens appear for a picnic, and are shocked to find a pirate in their midst. With **"Oh, Is There Not One Maiden Breast,"** Frederic pleads that one of the maidens may take pity on him. Just when it appears that all will reject him, Mabel appears and bravely offers him her heart. The other pirates spot the lovely maidens and creep in to kidnap them. The girls' father, the Major-General appears, hoping to foil the pirates' plans of marriage. He plays on his knowledge that Pirates of Penzance are orphans and are always tenderhearted toward other orphans, explaining that he too is an orphan and would be lost and lonely without his daughters. The pirates relent and the Major-General, Frederic and the girls depart, leaving poor Ruth with the pirates.

Act II opens in a ruined chapel, where the Major-General confesses to Frederic and Mabel that he is not actually an orphan. Frederic explains his plans to put the pirates out of business, and is in the process of proposing to Mabel when policemen arrive on their way to conquer the pirates themselves. They are just describing their grand plans when Ruth and the Pirate King arrive with a most ingenious paradox. Apparently Frederic was born on a leap-year day, so he won't actually reach his 21st birthday until 1940. Therefore he is still the pirates' apprentice. Always a slave to duty, Frederic returns to his pirate life, where honor forces him to tell the pirates that the Major-General is not an orphan. The policemen reappear and reluctantly prepare to arrest the pirates. The pirates meanwhile can be heard sneaking up on the Major-General. Just as the pirates are about to do in the Major-General, the policemen leap to his defense, only to be defeated almost immediately. They are about to be killed when the police pull Union Jacks from their pockets and command the pirates to stand down in the name of Queen Victoria. The pirates, who love their Queen, comply. Ruth puts everything to rights by explaining that the pirates are actually noblemen who have gone wrong. They are immediately forgiven and given back their titles. Frederic and Mabel reunite and the Major-General asks the pirates/nobles to marry his daughters.

PRINCESS IDA

or *Castle Adamant*
First produced at the Savoy Theatre, London, on January 5, 1884, with an initial run of 246 performances. *Princess Ida* is the only three-act operetta by Gilbert and Sullivan.

This satire on women's suffrage and Darwin's evolutionary theories opens on a scene of great expectation. Prince Hilarion awaits the arrival of Princess Ida, to whom he has been betrothed since infancy. Hilarion sings **"Twenty Years Ago,"** reminiscing about the couple's last meeting, when he was only two years old and she was but a twelve-month-old. Ida's father, King Gama, arrives without her, explaining to the Prince and his father King Hildebrand that Princess Ida is now running a school for girls at Castle Adamant. There they study the classics and the villainy of men. Hildebrand and Hilarion decide to hold Gama and his three sons as hostages while they storm the Castle Adamant to claim the Princess.

Hilarion and his friends Cyril and Florian scale the castle wall and disguise themselves in women's clothing. With several of the women aware of the men, and keeping their secret, the three pull off the ruse for a time. But after drinking a bit too much, Cyril bursts into song with **"Would You Know the Kind of Maid,"** and gives up the secret. Princess Ida orders the men's arrest. But King Hildebrand has massed his troops outside the castle walls to force Ida to make good on the betrothal. He gives her twenty-four hours to make up her mind, threatening to raze the castle and hang her brothers and father if she declines.

The Princess decides to fight, but her students are in terror of hurting someone so they refuse. Meanwhile King Hildebrand has decided that fighting women is in poor form, so he has Ida's brothers brought from his castle to fight for the women against Prince Hilarion and his two friends. Hilarion and company win. Princess Ida marries Hilarion, and two of her colleagues marry his friends. Lady Blanche is left to fulfill her dream of running the school and the curtain falls.

RUDDIGORE

or *The Witch's Curse*

First produced at the Savoy Theatre, London, on March 14, 1885, an initial run of 288 performances.

The professional bridesmaids in the Cornish village of Rederring are antsy for work. The lovely Rose Maybud is the most likely candidate, but she keeps rejecting suitors. She explains that she is waiting for the right person. Rose's Aunt Hannah tells of Sir Roderic Murgatroyd of Ruddigore, her lost love. Roderic defied the curse of the Murgatroyd heirs, which condemns them to commit a crime each day or perish, and died on their wedding day. Despard Murgatroyd has assumed the title and is living the obligatory life of crime. The shy Robin Oakapple, who is really Sir Ruthven Murgatroyd, appears. Robin explains that he is too shy to approach Rose. Robin's half brother, Richard, returns home and tells of his life as a sailor with **"I Shipped, D'Ye See."** Richard offers to woo Rose on Robin's behalf, but falls madly in love with her and woos her for himself instead. When Robin learns of this betrayal, he poisons Rose's mind against sailors and she turns her affections to him. At this point, Mad Margaret enters. Driven to insanity by her passion for Despard, she is wildly jealous of Rose, who reassures her. The plot thickens when Robin reveals himself as Despard's older brother, whom all thought was dead. Robin's title is restored and Rose leaves him for Despard. But Despard spurns her, going back to Margaret. Rose returns to Richard and Robin collapses.

Act II opens with a haggard Sir Ruthven (Robin) in the picture gallery of his castle, looking for a crime to commit. Rose and Richard have come to ask permission to marry and Ruthven threatens to imprison Rose as his crime of the day. Richard pulls out a Union Jack, which of course even the worst of criminals cannot ignore, and the two leave safely. At this point, the portraits of the previously cursed Murgatroyds come to life to remind Ruthven what will happen if he fails to commit a crime. Ruthven wearily sends someone off to kidnap a maiden on his behalf, which brings Hannah to the castle. In the meantime Despard and Margaret, now school masters, arrive to encourage Ruthven to reform. They add that under the law Ruthven is responsible for Despard's crime as well as his own. Ruthven vows to reform, no matter what the consequences. With Hannah in the room, Ruthven calls upon the picture of his Uncle Roderic to help him. Roderic's picture comes to life and he spots Hannah. Ruthven leaves, contemplating his predicament. But the day is saved when Ruthven rushes back in with a brainstorm. Failing to commit a crime each day while knowing the sentence for such action is death, he reasons, is tantamount to suicide. Since suicide is a crime in and of itself, Sir Roderic should never have died. This means that all concerned may pair off as they see fit and thus ends the curse and the operetta.

THE SORCERER

First produced at the Opéra Comique, London, on November 17, 1877, with an initial run of 178 performances.

The village of Ploverleigh is percolating with affection as this satire on Victorian society opens. Villager Constance Partlet harbors secret feelings for Dr. Daly, the Vicar, but Daly is oblivious of Constance's feelings. Constance's mother, meanwhile, has her eye on the Notary. Aline Sangazure glories in her engagement to Alexis Poindextre of the Grenadier Guards. Alexis describes his ideal love, singing **"For Love Alone."** Aline and Alexis, hoping to share their loving bliss with the entire village, hire a sorcerer to drug the community with a love-at-first-sight potion. The potion is administered through tea at a village picnic. Everyone but the young lovers and the sorcerer drinks the potion-spiked tea and falls into a deep sleep.

As midnight strikes the villagers begin to awaken, immediately falling head-over-heels in love with the first person they happen to spot. Seeing the potion's effects, Alexis asks Aline to drink the potion, to deepen their love for each other. She refuses, causing a quarrel; Alexis rebuffs her, singing **"It Is Not**

Love." Eventually she agrees to drink the potion, but spots Dr. Daly immediately afterward and falls in love with him instead of her betrothed Alexis. The potion-induced romances have made a mess of things. Alexis' father, Sir Marmaduke has fallen for Mrs. Partlet, while Lady Sangazure has become smitten with Mr. Wells and Constance with the Notary. It becomes apparent that either Alexis or Mr. Wells must give his life to the forces of evil to break the spell. Neither is willing so a vote is taken. The sorcerer loses and is swallowed up by the earth as a gong sounds. The potion's spell is broken and the villagers return to their original affections.

TRIAL BY JURY

First produced at the Royalty Theatre, London, on March 25, 1875, with an initial run of 131 performances. It appeared on a triple bill, with Offenbach's *La Périchole* as the centerpiece. It was an immediate hit, and soon became the main attraction. The brief *Trial By Jury* is sometimes performed with *HMS Pinafore*.

Sullivan's only one-act opera and the writers' only collaborative work with no spoken dialogue, *Trial by Jury* opens on a courtroom where a trial for breach of marital promise is about to begin. An usher admonishes the jurors to be impartial but then tells them to listen with sympathy to Angelina, the spurned bride, and to ignore the story of Edwin, the would-be groom. The jurors shake their fists at Edwin. They make it clear they are not interested as he explains how he fell in and out of love with Angelina, with **"When First My Old, Old Love I Knew."** The judge enters, promptly singing his entire life's story for the court. When the bridesmaids enter, dressed for the wedding, the judge immediately sends a note to one of them, professing his love for her. Angelina enters shortly, in her wedding gown. The judge immediately has the amorous note taken from the bridesmaid and given to Angelina. The trial quickly degenerates into a weeping bride clinging to the groom who still rejects her. Edwin makes a plea to the jury with **"Oh, Gentlemen, Listen, I Pray,"** but the judge ends the trial and the operetta by announcing that he will marry Angelina himself.

UTOPIA LIMITED

or *The Flowers of Progress*
First produced at the Savoy Theatre, London, on October 7, 1893, with an initial run of 245 performances.

This mockery of Victorian society is set on the fictitious South Pacific island of Utopia, where the King's daughter, Princess Zara, is about to return from school in Britain. Two wise men, Scaphio and Phantis, hold power over Utopia and its King. The two wise men tout their own virtues. Tarara explains that as the Public Exploder he must explode anything or anyone denounced by Scaphio and Phantis. A scandal sheet called the *Palace Peeper* has accused the King of terrible behavior and Tarara thinks it is time for an explosion. The King announces that due to public demand Utopia will be modeled after Great Britain, with Lady Sophy teaching the girls proper behavior. We learn that the King himself has written the scandal sheet, under orders from Scaphio and Phantis. Scaphio has promised Phantis to help him win Zara's heart. But one look at her and he is in love with her himself. Zara and Fitzbattleaxe interrupt, explaining that in Britain if two men love one woman they must duel to the death to decide who wins the woman.

As Act II begins, Fitzbattleaxe asks his beloved Zara to bear with him as he sings **"A Tenor, All Singers Above,"** for the fervor of his love affects his voice. The King tells Zara of Scaphio and Phantis' power over him. She has conveniently brought "experts" from England to set Utopia to rights. As per their advice, the King incorporates himself. In fact, everyone in Utopia is now a limited company. The King, dressed in British military attire, holds his first cabinet meeting. With Scaphio and Phantis grumbling about the Anglicization of Utopia, the King tells them he is a limited company and therefore immune to their control. They call in the Public Exploder and cook up a plot. The King tells Lady Sophy the truth about the *Palace Peeper* and about Scaphio and Phantis. But things are now too good in Utopia. There is no work for the Army or Navy, no disease for doctors to cure and no crime for lawyers to prosecute. So the King decides to follow the British system of Government by party saying, "No political measures will endure, because one party will assuredly undo all that the other party has done."

THE YEOMEN OF THE GUARD
or *The Merryman and His Maid*
First produced at the Savoy Theatre, London, on October 3, 1888, with an initial run of 423 performances.

The year is fifteen-hundred-and-something. Young Phoebe Meryll ponders the heartbreaks of love. She is pining for the dashing Colonel Fairfax who sits in the Tower of London awaiting execution for the crime of sorcery, singing **"Is Life a Boon?"** He was accused of the crime by his scheming cousin. Should he die without a wife, Fairfax explains to the Lieutenant, his title and wealth transfer to the cousin. He begs the Lieutenant to marry him to the poorest woman that can be found so that she might inherit his name and wealth instead. Meanwhile Wilfred, Head Jailor and Assistant Tormentor of the Tower of London, has eyes for Phoebe. While she once thought him fine, she has since become enamored of the Colonel and will have nothing to with Wilfred. Jester Jack Point and singer Elsie Maynard enter. A less than appreciative crowd threatens to mob them but the Lieutenant saves them, immediately marrying Elsie to Fairfax. Jack describes his profession. Meanwhile, Phoebe has come up with a plan. She flirts with Wilfrid and steals his keys just long enough for her father to free Fairfax. Wilfrid is barely gone when Fairfax appears in the uniform of the Yeomen of the Guard, posing as the son of Sergeant Meryll. As Phoebe and her "brother" give each other an uncommonly affectionate greeting, the bells toll the hour of the execution. Guards rush back with the news that Fairfax has escaped.

Act II finds Jack Point feeling regret for allowing Elsie to marry Fairfax. It seemed a better idea when Fairfax was about to die, since Jack wanted to marry Elsie himself and figured Fairfax's money would be welcome. He advises Wilfrid on the hazards of jesting. The newly freed Fairfax is putting the fidelity of his new wife to the test, masquerading as Leonard Meryll. Jack and Wilfrid conspire to fake Fairfax's death, saying that they shot the Colonel as he dove into the river. With Fairfax thought dead, Jack proposes to Elsie, who rejects him. Fairfax sings **"Free From His Fetters Grim,"** wondering who his new bride might be, only to discover moments later that his bride is Elsie. Phoebe, distraught over loosing Fairfax tells Wilfrid of the escape and disguise. Wilfrid forces her to marry him to keep the secret. Suddenly the real Leonard appears with an official pardon for Fairfax. Elsie, at first heartbroken to learn that her real husband is alive is delighted when it is revealed that her beloved Leonard is really Fairfax and therefore they are married. Jack, the only one left without a spouse, falls to the ground in a faint.

Gilbert & Sullivan for Singers

Tenor

Take a Pair of Sparkling Eyes

THE GONDOLIERS

Words by W.S. Gilbert
Music by Arthur Sullivan

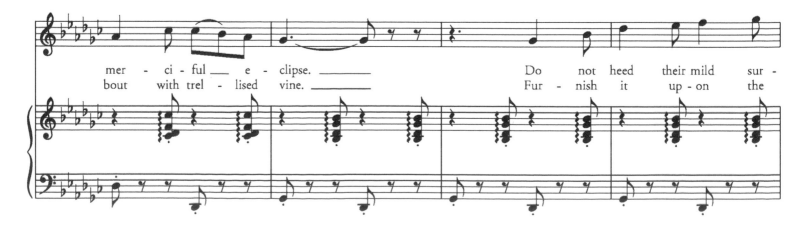

prise, _____ Hav-ing passed the Ru - bi - con. _____ Take a pair of ros - y
spot _____ With the trea - sures rich and rare _____ I've en - deav - oured to _ de -

lips. _____ Take a fig - ure trim - ly planned, _ Such as
fine. _____ Live to love and love to live— _ You will

ad - mi - ra - tion whets _ (Be par - tic - u - lar in this); Take a
ri - pen at your ease, _ Grow-ing on the sun - ny side— Fate has

ten - der lit - tle hand, _ Fringed with dain - ty fin - ger - ettes, _ Press _____
noth - ing more to give. _ You're a dain - ty man to please _ if _____

14

can! _____   Take my coun - sel, hap - py man!

Act up - on it, if you can,   if you can,   if you

cresc.   *f*   *con forza*

can,   Act up - on it, if you can, _____ hap - py man,

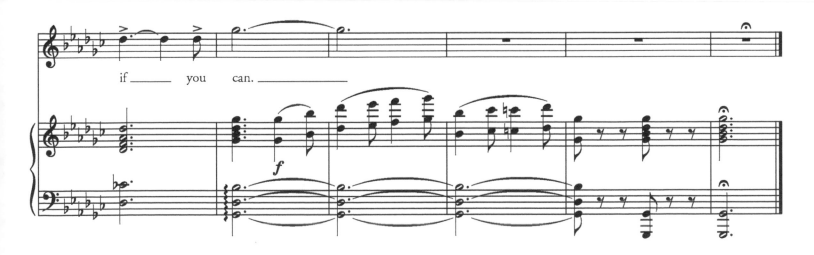

if _____ you can. _____

Rising Early in the Morning

THE GONDOLIERS

Words by W.S. Gilbert
Music by Arthur Sullivan

bark with - out de - lay On the du - ties of the day. First, we

pol - ish off some batch - es Of po - lit - i - cal des - patch - es, And

lunch - eon (mak - ing mer - ry On a bun and glass of sher - ry), If we've

for - eign pol - i - ti - cians cir - cum - vent; Then, if bus' - ness is - n't heav - y, We may

noth - ing in par - tic - u - lar to do, We may make a Proc - la - ma - tion, Or re -

hold a Roy - al lev - ée, Or rat - i - fy some Acts of Par - lia - ment. Then we

ceive a Dep - u - ta - tion—Then we pos - si - bly cre - ate a Peer or two. Then we

prob - a - bly re - view the house - hold troops— With the
help a fel - low - crea - ture on his path With the

u - sual "Shal-loo humps!" and "Shal-loo hoops!" Or re - ceive with cer - e - mo - ni - al and
Gar - ter, or the This - tle, or the Bath. Or we dress and tod - dle off in sem - i -

1st time ff 2nd time pp

state An in - ter - est - ing East - ern po - ten -
State To a fes - ti - val, a func - tion, or a

tate. Af - ter that we gen - er - al - ly Go and dress our pri - vate
fête. Then we go and stand as sen - try At the Pal - ace (pri - vate

* lower notes are for the second verse

val - et— (It's a rath - er ner - vous du - ty— he's a touch - y lit - tle
en - try), March - ing hith - er, march - ing thith - er, up and down and to and

man)— Write some let - ters lit - er - a - ry For our pri - vate sec - re -
fro, While the war - ri - or on du - ty Goes in search of beer and

ta - ry— He is shak - y in his spell - ing, so we help him if we can. Then, in
beau - ty (And it gen - er - al - ly hap - pens that he has - n't far to go). He re -

view of crav - ings in - ner, We go down and or - der din - ner; Then we
lieves us, if he's a - ble, Just in time to lay the ta - ble, Then we

pol - ish the re - ga - lia and the cor - o - na - tion plate— Spend an
dine and serve the cof - fee, and at half - past twelve or one, With a

hour in tit - i - vat - ing All our Gen - tle - men - in - Wait - ing; Or we
pleas - ure that's em - phat - ic We re - tire_____ to our at - tic With the

run on lit - tle er - rands for the Min - is - ters of State. Oh, _____ phi
grat - i - fy - ing feel - ing that our du - ty has been done! Oh, _____ phi -

los - o - phers may sing Of the trou - bles of a King; Yet the
los - o - phers may sing Of the trou - bles of a King; But of

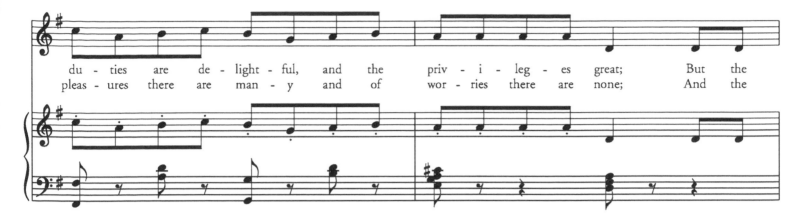

duties are de - light - ful, and the priv - i - leg - es great; But the
pleas - ures there are man - y and of wor - ries there are none; And the

priv - i - lege and pleas - ure That we treas - ure be - yond meas - ure Is to
cul - mi - nat - ing pleas - ure That we treas - ure be - yond meas - ure Is the

run on lit - tle er - rands for the Min - is - ters of State. Oh, _____ phi -
grat - i - fy - ing feel - ing that our du - ty has been done! Oh, _____ phi -

los - o - phers may sing Of the trou - bles of a King; Yet the
los - o - phers may sing Of the trou - bles of a King; But of

du - ties are de - light - ful, and the priv - i - leg - es great; But the
pleas - ures there are man - y, and of wor - ries there are none; And the

priv - i - lege and pleas - ure That we treas - ure be - yond meas - ure Is to
cul - mi - nat - ing pleas - ure That we treas - ure be - yond meas - ure Is the

run on lit - tle er - rands for the Min - is - ters of State. Af - ter
grat - i - fy - ing feel - ing that our

du - ty has been done!

A Maiden Fair to See

HMS PINAFORE

Words by W.S. Gilbert
Music by Arthur Sullivan

that which love has taught (For love had been his tu - tor); Oh,

pit - y, pit - y me— Our cap - tain's daugh - ter, she; And I, that low - ly

suit - or! Oh, pit - y, pit - y me— Our cap-tain's daugh-ter she; And I, that low - ly

suit - or!

Fair Moon, to Thee I Sing

HMS PINAFORE

Words by W.S. Gilbert
Music by Arthur Sullivan

Moderato

CAPTAIN CORCORAN:

Fair moon, to thee ___ I ___ sing, Bright re-gent of the

heav - ens, Say, why is ev-'ry-thing ___

Ei - ther at six - es or at sev - ens? Say, why is

ev - 'ry - thing ____ Ei - ther at six - es or at sev - ens? I have

lived hith - er - to Free from the breath __ of ____

slan - der, Be - loved by all my crew, A

real - ly pop-u-lar com-mand - er. But now my kind-ly crew re-

bel, _____ My daugh-ter to a tar is par - tial, Sir

Jo - seph storms, and, sad to tell, He threat - ens _____ a court -

mar - tial! Fair moon, to thee _ I _____ sing,

Bright re - gent of the heav - ens, Say, why is

ev - 'ry - thing Ei - ther at six - es or at sev - ens?

Fair moon, to thee I sing, Bright re - gent of the

colla voce

heavens!

a tempo *p*

Spurn Not the Nobly Born
IOLANTHE

Words by W.S. Gilbert
Music by Arthur Sullivan

LORD TOLLOLLER:

Spurn not the no-bly born With love af-fect-ed, Nor treat with vir-tuous scorn The well-con-nect-ed! High rank in-volves no shame, We boast an e-qual claim With him of hum-ble name To be res-pect-ed! Blue blood, blue blood! When vir-tuous love is sought Thy

pow - er is ____ naught, Though dat - ing from the Flood, Blue blood, _____ ah, blue blood!

Spare us the bit - ter pain Of stern __ de - ni - als, Nor with low - born dis - dain Aug -

ment __ our __ tri - als; Hearts just as pure and fair May beat in Bel - grave Square

As in the low-ly air Of Sev-en Di-als! Blue blood, blue blood! Of

what a-vail art thou To serve ___ us ___ now? Though dat-ing from the Flood, Blue blood, ___

___ ah, blue blood!

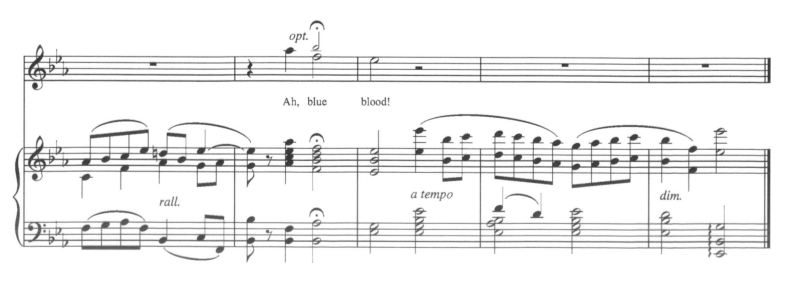

Ah, blue blood!

A Wand'ring Minstrel I

THE MIKADO

Words by W.S. Gilbert
Music by Arthur Sullivan

cat - a - logue is long, Thro' ev - 'ry pas - sion rang - ing, And

to your hu - mours chang - ing I tune my sup - ple song!

I tune my sup - ple song!

Andante expressivo

p

Are you in sen - ti - men - tal mood? I'll sigh with you, Oh,

Allegro marziale ♩ = 144

But if pa - tri-ot - ic sen - ti - ment is want - ed, I've pa - tri-ot - ic bal - lads cut and dried; For wher - e'er our coun - try ban - ner may be plant - ed, All oth - er lo - cal ban - ners are de - fied! Our war - ri-ors, in ser - ried ranks as - sem - bled, Nev - er

quail— or they con-ceal it if they do— And I should-n't be sur-prised if na - tions

trem - bled Be-fore the might - y troops, the troops — of Tit - i - pu! We should - n't be sur-prised if

na - tions trem - bled, trem - bled with a - larm be - fore the might - y troops, the troops — of Tit - i -

Allegro pesante, non troppo vivo ♪ = 160

pu! And if you call for a

sail - or ___ sees Is when he's down At an in - land ___ town, With his Nan - cy on his

knees, yeo - ho! And his arm ___ a - round her waist! Then man the cap - stan—

off we go, As the fid - dler swings us round, With a

yeo heave - ho, And a rum ___ be - low, Hur - rah for the home - ward

bound! _____ With a yeo heave - ho, _____ And a

f

rum be - low, _____ Yeo - ho, heave -

ho, Yeo - ho, heave - ho, heave - ho, heave - ho, yeo -

cresc.

ho!

ff

dim.

Allegretto come I°

Oh, Is There Not One Maiden Breast

THE PIRATES OF PENZANCE

Words by W.S. Gilbert
Music by Arthur Sullivan

will - ing-ly All mat - ri - mo - nial am - bi - tion, To res - cue such a

one as I From his un - for - tu - nate po - si - tion, From his _____ po -

si - tion, To res - cue such a one as I From his _____ un - for - tu -

nate po - si - tion?

Would You Know the Kind of Maid
PRINCESS IDA

Words by W.S. Gilbert
Music by Arthur Sullivan

Allegretto

CYRIL:

1. Would __ you know the kind __ of maid Sets __ my heart a - flame - a?

Eyes __ must be down - cast __ and staid, Cheeks __ must flush for shame __ a!

She may nei - ther dance nor sing, But, de - mure in ev - 'ry - thing,

Hang her head— in— mo - dest way, With pout - ing lips,————

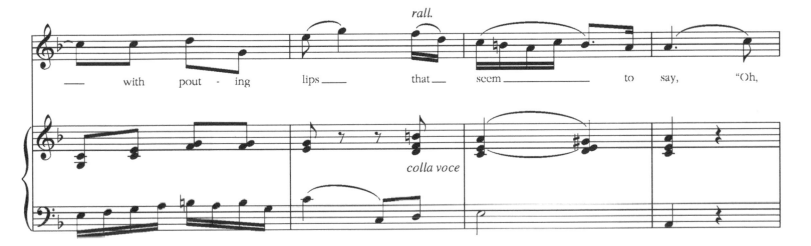

— with pout - ing lips— that— seem——— to say, "Oh,

rall.

colla voce

a tempo
p

kiss me, kiss me, kiss me, kiss me, Though— I— die of shame - a,"

a tempo

Please you, that's the kind of maid Sets— my heart a - flame - a!

"Kiss me, kiss me, kiss me, kiss me, Though __ I __ die of shame - a,"

cresc.

Please you, that's the kind of maid Sets __ my heart a - flame - a!

f

2. When __ a maid is

p

bold __ and gay, With __ a tongue goes clang - a, Flaun - ting it in

kiss me, kiss me, kiss me, kiss me, Though __ I __ die of shame - a!" Please you that's the

kind of maid Sets __ my heart a - flame - a! "Kiss me, kiss me, kiss me, kiss me,

Though __ I ___ die for shame - a!" Please you that's the kind of maid

Sets __ my heart __ a - flame - a!

Twenty Years Ago

PRINCESS IDA

Words by W.S. Gilbert
Music by Arthur Sullivan

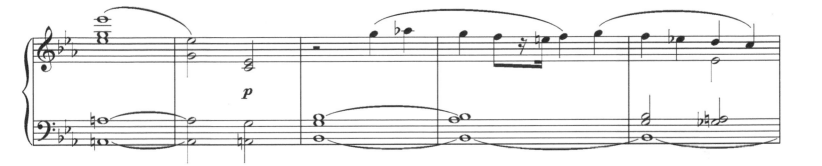

To - day we meet, My ba - by bride and I—

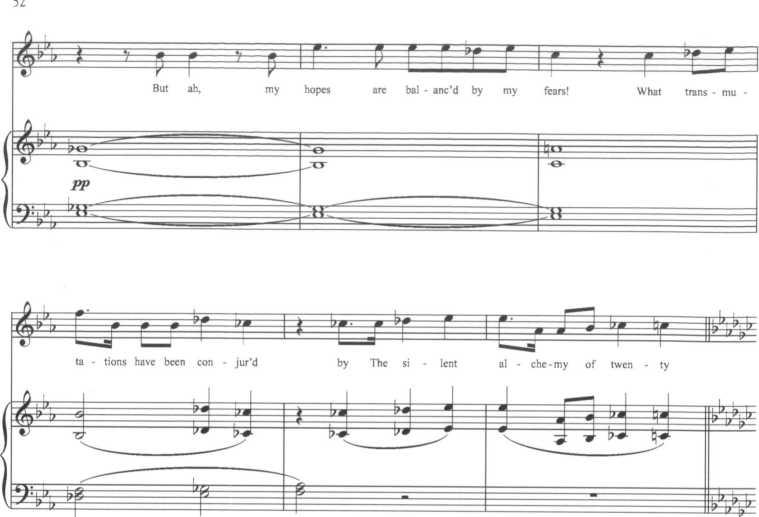

But ah, my hopes are bal-anc'd by my fears! What trans-mu-ta-tions have been con-jur'd by The si-lent al-che-my of twen-ty years!

Moderato

years!

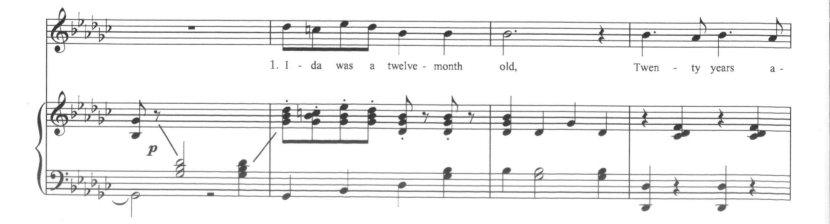

1. I-da was a twelve-month old, Twen-ty years a-

go!　　　　　　I was twice her age, I'm told,

Twen - ty years a - go!　　　Hus - band ___ twice ___ as ___

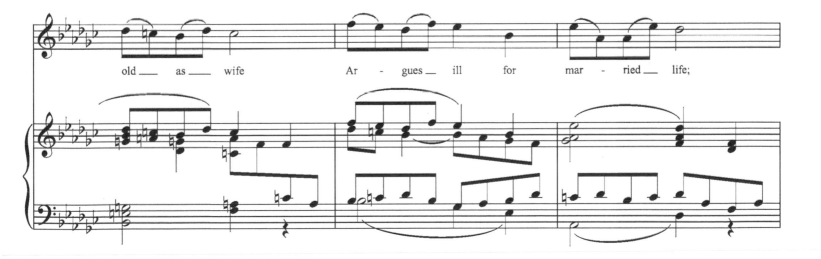

old ___ as ___ wife　Ar - gues ill for mar - ried ___ life;

Bale - ful ___ pro - phe - cies ___ were ___ rife,　Twen - ty years a -

54

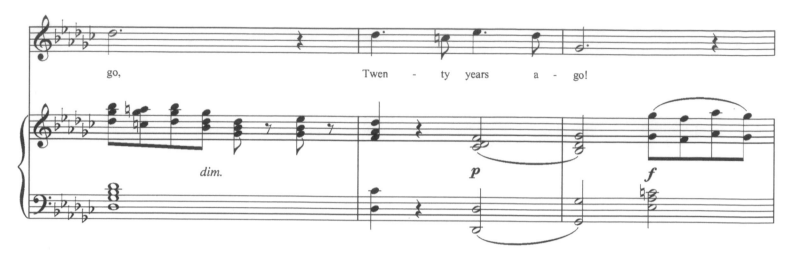

go,   Twen - ty years a - go!

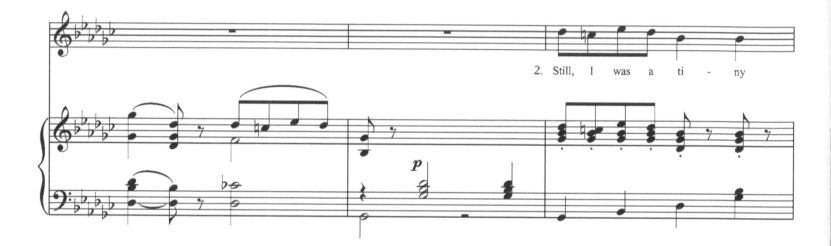

2. Still, I was a ti - ny

Prince   Twen - ty years a - go.

She has gain'd up - on me, since   Twen - ty years a -

go.   Though __ she's __ twen - ty - one, __ it's __ true.

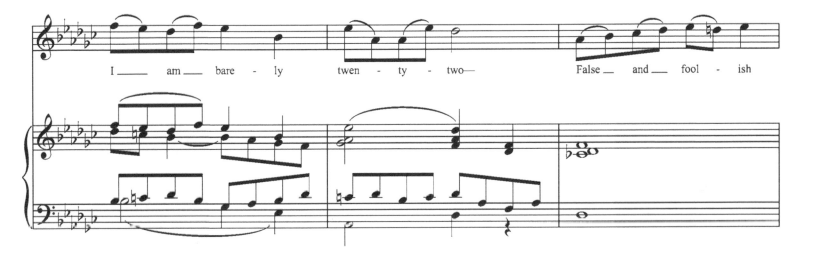

I __ am __ bare - ly   twen - ty - two—   False __ and __ fool - ish

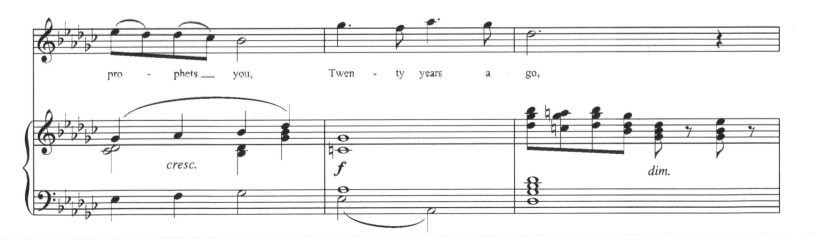

pro - phets __ you,   Twen - ty years a - go,

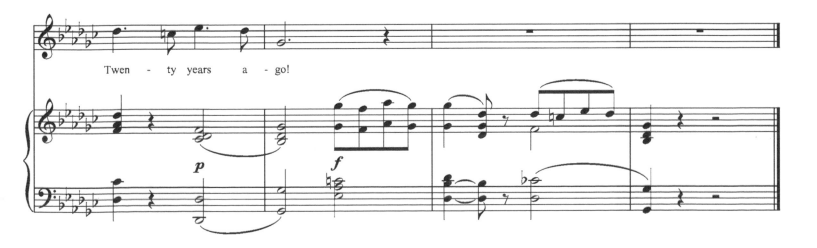

Twen - ty years a - go!

I Shipped, D'Ye See
RUDDIGORE

Words by W.S. Gilbert
Music by Arthur Sullivan

RICHARD:

1. I shipped, d'ye see, in a Rev - e - nue sloop, And, ___
Capt'n he up and he says, says he, "That ___
up with our helm, and we scuds be - fore the breeze, As we

off Cape Fin - is - tere, A mer - chant - man we see, A ___
chap we need not fear,— We can take her, if we like, She is
gives a com - pas - sion - at - ing cheer; Frog gee an - swers with a shout As he

French - man, go - ing free, So we made for the bold Moun - seer, D'ye _ see? We
sar - tin for to strike, For she's on - ly a darned Moun - seer, D'ye _ see? She's
sees us go a - bout, Which was grate - ful of the poor Moun - seer, D'ye _ see? Which was

made for the bold Moun - seer. But she proved to be a Frig - ate, and she
on - ly a darned Moun - seer! But to fight a French fal - lal— it's like
grate - ful of the poor Moun - seer! And I'll wa - ger in their joy they _

up _ with her ports, And _ fires with a thir - ty - two! It
hit - tin' of a gal,— It's a lub - ber - ly thing for to do; For
kissed each oth - er's cheek (Which is what them fur ri ners _ do), And they

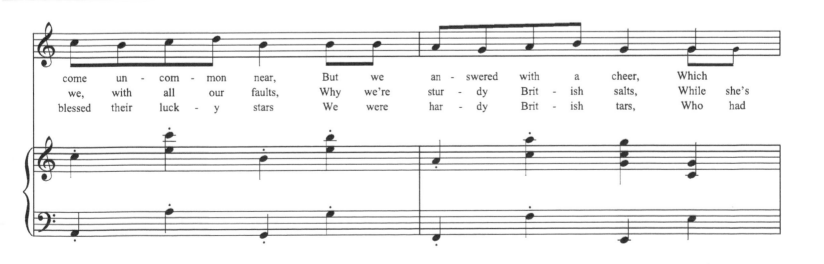

come un - com - mon near, But we an - swered with a cheer, Which
we, with all our faults, Why we're stur - dy Brit - ish salts, While she's
blessed their luck - y stars We were har - dy Brit - ish tars, Who had

For Love Alone

THE SORCERER

Words by W.S. Gilbert
Music by Arthur Sullivan

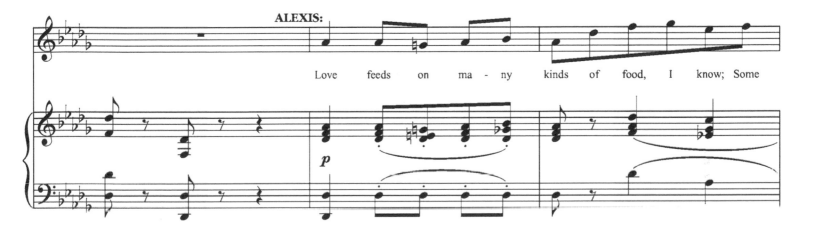

Love feeds on ma-ny kinds of food, I know; Some

love for rank, and some for du-ty; Some give their hearts a-

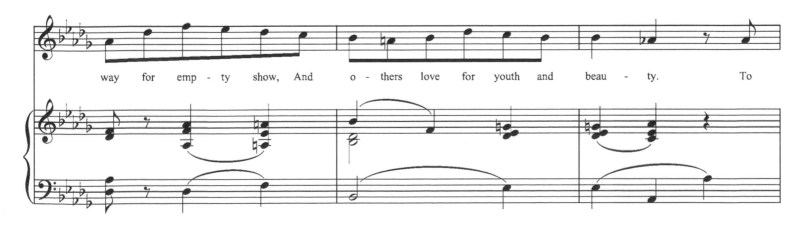

way for emp-ty show, And o-thers love for youth and beau-ty. To

love for mon - ey all the world is prone; Some love them - selves, and live all

lone - ly; Give me the love that loves for love a -

lone— I love that love, I love it on - ly! I love that

love, I love it on - ly! Give me the love that loves for

love a - lone— I love that love, I love it on -

f

colla voce

ly!

ff

dim.

What man for a - ny

p

o - ther joy can thirst, Whose lov - ing wife a - dores him du - ly?

Want, mi - se - ry, and Care may work their worst, If lov - ing wo - man loves you

tru - ly. A lov - er's thoughts are e - ver with his own— None

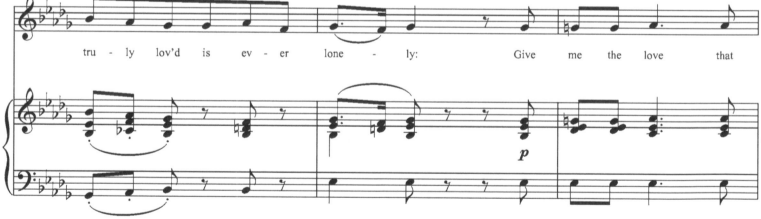

tru - ly lov'd is ev - er lone - ly: Give me the love that

loves for love a - lone— I love that love, I love it

on - ly! I love that love, I love it on - ly! Give

me the love that loves for love a - lone— I love that love, I love it

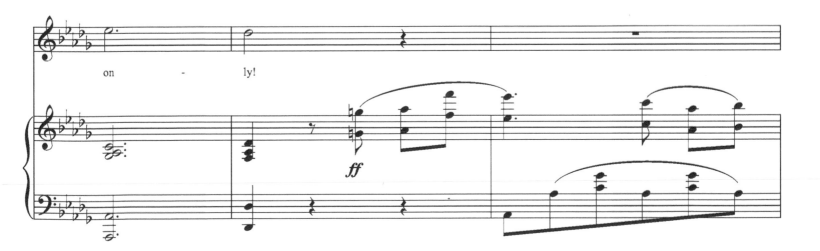

on - ly!

It Is Not Love
THE SORCERER

Words by W.S. Gilbert
Music by Arthur Sullivan

Allegro con brio

ALEXIS:

Thou hast the pow'r thy vaun - ted love To sanc - ti - fy, all

doubt a - bove, De - spite the gath - 'ring shade; To

make that love of thine so sure That, come what may, it

fades with - in the hour; _____ If such thy

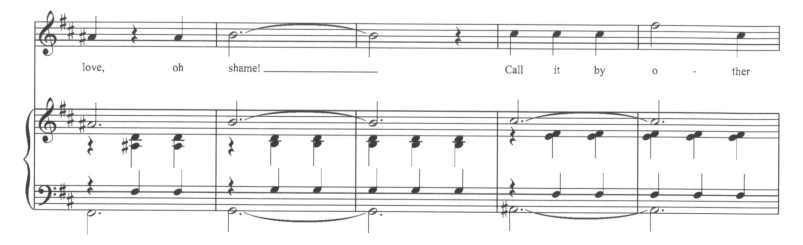

love, oh shame! _____ Call it by o - ther

name, It is not love! _____ It is not

Tempo I

love!

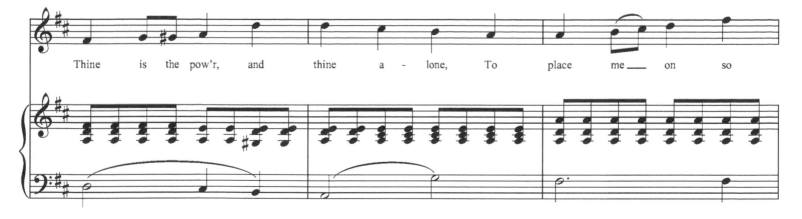

Thine is the pow'r, and thine a - lone, To place me __ on so

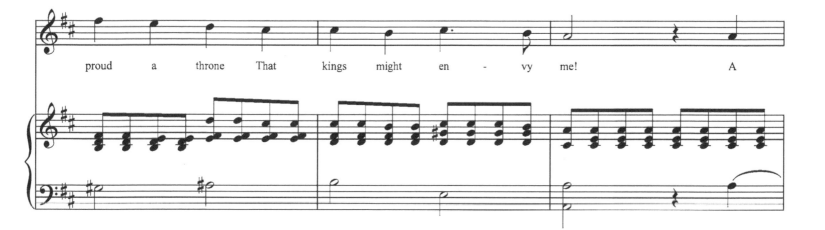

proud a throne That kings might en - vy me! A

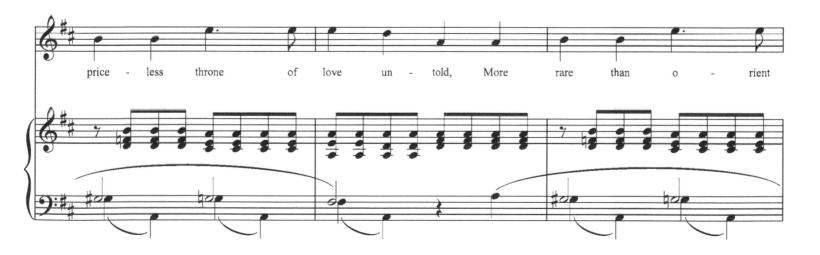

price - less throne of love un - told, More rare than o - rient

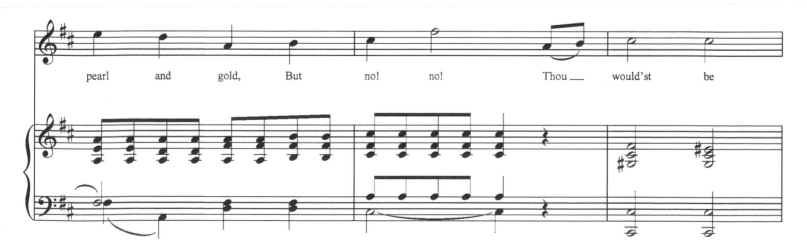

pearl and gold, But no! no! Thou __ would'st be

Tempo di valse
dolce

free! Such love is like the ray _____ That

dies with - in the day; _____ If such thy

love, oh shame! _____ Call it by o - ther name. _____

_____ Such love is like the ray _____ That dies with -

Oh, Gentlemen, Listen, I Pray

TRIAL BY JURY

Words by W.S. Gilbert
Music by Arthur Sullivan

Allegretto non troppo vivace

DEFENDANT:

Oh, gen - tle - men, lis - ten, I pray, Tho' I own that my
can - not eat break - fast all day, ___ Nor is it the

heart has been rang - ing, Of na - ture the laws I o - bey, For na - ture is
act of a sin - ner, When break - fast is tak - en a - way, To turn his at -

con - stant - ly chang - ing: The moon in her phas - es is found, The time and the
ten - tion to din - ner; And it's not in the range of be - lief To look up - on

wind and the weath - er, The months in suc - ces - sion come round, And you don't find two
him as a glut - ton Who, when he is tired of beef, De - ter - mines to

rall.   *a tempo*

Mon - days to - geth - er. Ah! Con - sid - er the mor - al, I
tac - kle the mut - ton. Ah! But this I am will - ing to

rall.   *a tempo*

cresc.

pray, Nor bring a young fel - low to sor - row, Who loves this young la - dy to -
say, If it will ap - pease her sor - row, I'll mar - ry this la - dy to -

cresc.

day,   And loves that young la — dy to - mor-row!   Con - sid - er the mor - al, we
day, And I'll mar — ry the oth — er to - mor-row!   But this he is will - ing to

pray,   Nor bring a young fel - low to sor - row,   Who loves this young la - dy to -
say,   If it will ap - pease — her sor - row,   He'll mar - ry this la - dy to -

day,   And loves that young la — dy to - mor-row!   You
day, And he'll mar - ry the oth — er to - mor-row!

When First My Old, Old Love I Knew

TRIAL BY JURY

Words by W.S. Gilbert
Music by Arthur Sullivan

74

feet ___ I threw, I was a love - sick boy! No
bore ___ in - tense Un - to her love - sick boy! With

terms seem'd too ___ ex - trav - a - gant Up - on her to ___ em -
fit - ful glim - mer burnt my flame, And I grew cold ___ and

ploy; ___ I used to mope, ___ and sigh, and pant,
coy, ___ At last, one morn - ing, I be - came An -

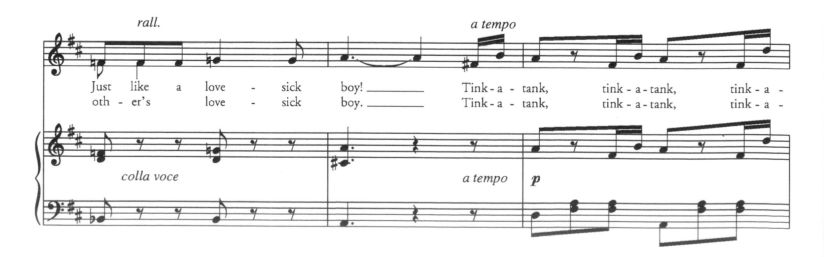

Just like a love - sick boy! ___ Tink - a - tank, tink - a - tank, tink - a -
oth - er's love - sick boy. ___ Tink - a - tank, tink - a - tank, tink - a -

tank,   Tink-a-tank, tink-a-tank, tink-a-tank,   I
tank,   Tink-a-tank, tink-a-tank, tink-a-tank,   At

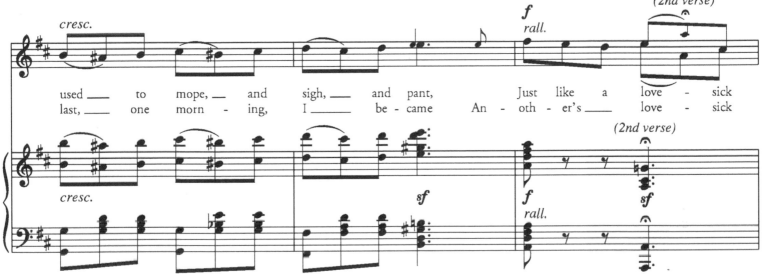

used ___ to mope, ___ and sigh, ___ and pant, Just like a love - sick
last, ___ one morn - ing, I ___ be - came An - oth - er's ___ love - sick

boy.
boy.

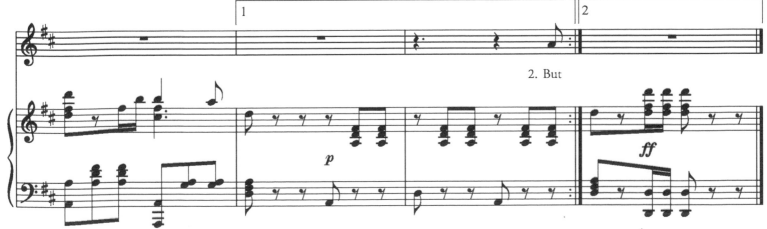

2. But

A Tenor, All Singers Above
UTOPIA LIMITED

Words by W.S. Gilbert
Music by Arthur Sullivan

Allegretto a la serenata

Oh, Za - ra, my be - loved one, bear with me! Ah, do not laugh at my at - tempt - ed C! Re - pent not, mock - ing maid, thy girl - hood's choice— The fer - vour of my love af - fects my voice!

opt.

[colla voce]

Allegretto

1. A ten - or, all sing - ers a-
sing, if my fer - vour were

bove, (This does - n't ad - mit of a ques - tion), Should
mock, It's ea - sy e - nough if you're act - ing— But

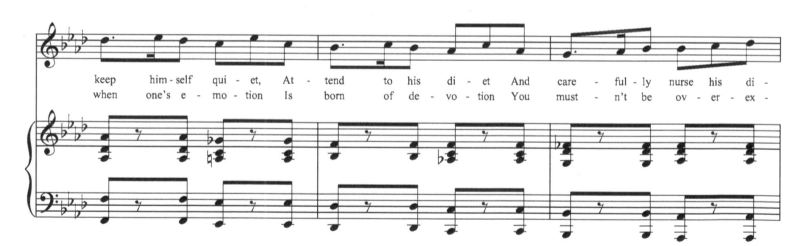

keep him - self qui - et, At - tend to his di - et And care - ful - ly nurse his di-
when one's e - mo - tion Is born of de - vo - tion You must - n't be ov - er - ex-

ges - tion: But when he is mad - ly in love It's
act - ing. One ought to be firm as a rock To

ten - or can't do him - self jus - tice.
ten - or can't do him - self jus - tice. *(Spoken:)* Now ob - serve— Ah!—

You see, I can't do my - self jus - tice!

2. I could

(ah!) It's no use— I can't do my - self jus - tice!

Free from His Fetters Grim

THE YEOMEN OF THE GUARD

Words by W.S. Gilbert
Music by Arthur Sullivan

For good and ill; Ah, is not one so tied A

rit. *freely*

pris - 'ner still, A pris - 'ner still? Ah, is not one so

rit. *dim.* *p*

a tempo

tied A pris - 'ner still?

f *a tempo*

Free, yet in fet - ters held Till his last hour, Gyves that no

smith can weld, No rust __ de - vour! Al - though a mon - arch's hand

Had set him free, Of all the cap - tive band __ The sad - dest

he, The sad - dest he! Of all the cap - tive band __ The

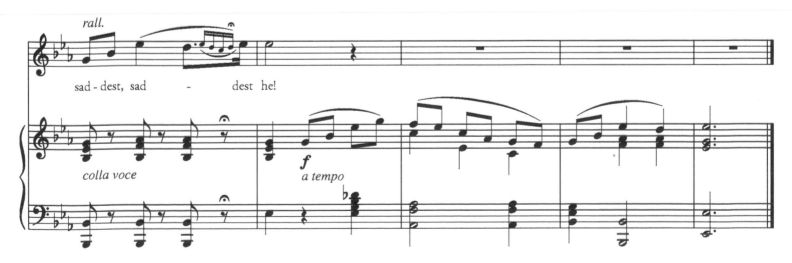

sad - dest, sad - dest he!

Is Life a Boon?
THE YEOMEN OF THE GUARD

Words by W.S. Gilbert
Music by Arthur Sullivan

live _____ An - oth - er moon! What kind of plaint have I, Who

un poco rit. *a tempo*

per - ish in Ju - ly, Who per - ish in Ju - ly? I might have had to

colla voce *a tempo*

die, _____ Per-chance, in June! I might have had to die, _____ Per -

chance, in June!

2. Is life a thorn? Then count it not a

whit! Nay, count it not a whit! Man is well done _____ with

it; Soon _____ as he's born He should all means es-

say To put the plague a - way; And I, war -

worn, Poor cap - tured fu - gi - tive, My life most glad - ly ___

give— I might have had to live ___ an - oth - er

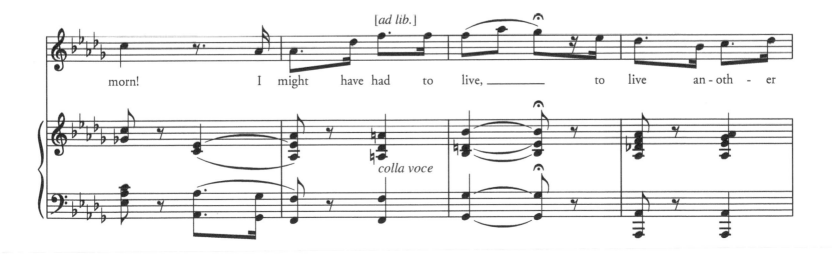

morn! I might have had to live, ___ to live an - oth - er

morn!